E OCEAN IN YOUR BATHTUB

BY Seth Fishman

ILLUSTRATED BY Isabel Greenberg

Greenwillow Books
An Imprint of HarperCollins *Publishers*

Library of Congress Cataloging-in-Publication Data is available.

Names: Fishman, Seth, author. | Greenberg, Isabel, illustrator.
Title: The ocean in your bathtub / by Seth Fishman ;
photographs by Isabel Greenberg.
Description: First edition. | New York : Greenwillow Books,
an imprint of HarperCollins Publishers, [2020] |
Audience: Ages 4–8 | Audience: Grades 2–3 |
Summary: "The Earth's five oceans and its water cycle connect all of us in
important and unexpected ways"— Provided by publisher.
Identifiers: LCCN 2019041850 | ISBN 9780062953360 (hardcover)
Subjects: LCSH: Ocean—Juvenile literature.
Classification: LCC GC21.5 .F56 2020 | DDC 551.46—dc23
LC record available at https://lccn.loc.gov/2019041850

20 21 22 23 24 ROT 10 9 8 7 6 5 4 3 2 1
First Edition

GREENWILLOW BOOKS

For Marget, who is my anything—S. F.

Would you do me a favor?

Check to see if there's any
salt water beneath you.

It's true!

ARCTIC OCEAN

PACIFIC
OCEAN

INDIAN
OCEAN

Five oceans cover
71 percent of our planet
and contain 97 percent
of our water.

Almost four out of
every ten humans
live within 60 miles of
one of those oceans.

EVAPORATION

CONDEN

That cloud (most likely) is loaded with water vapor STRAIGHT FROM THE OCEAN.

Sea water evaporated into the air and formed the cloud

and now it is drifting over you.

PRECIPITATION

Eventually, it will pour down rain.

And lots of that rain will

trickle back to the ocean

to form a new cloud.

We call this the **water cycle.**

Some water *doesn't* return directly to the ocean. It rains—or snows—down to fill our reservoirs and lakes and rivers. Those, along with underground aquifers, are our major sources of drinking water.

*The ocean is NOT a major source of drinking water— it's way too salty!

Every plant, tree, and blade of grass is fed by falling water. All our fruits, grains, and vegetables need water to grow, just like we do, and they make up a large part of the food we eat every day.

*Yep, the ocean's hiding in your afternoon snack!

In fact, those crops are only one part of the bounty of the sea.
About three billion people rely on seafood to survive.

The ocean doesn't just provide thunderstorms and drinking water and food for life on land. We actually BREATHE because of it, too. Even if you are too far from the sea to smell the salt, almost seven out of every ten gulps of air you take contain oxygen that comes from plant life in the ocean!

A "forest" of trillions and trillions of tiny plants *floats* in and on the sea, taking in sunlight and exhaling oxygen. They are like the big breathing lungs of the ocean.

*Never try to breathe while you are IN the ocean, unless you're wearing scuba or snorkeling gear!

Of course, humans aren't the only creatures relying on the oceans. Bears, birds, and numerous other animals rely on fish and seafood for their daily diet. Plants do too!

Soil along rivers that empty into the oceans is fertilized by fish that swim upriver. That's not even counting the (potentially many) more than one million species that live *in* the oceans.

The oceans are full of life and wonder.

Sand is formed by rock being smashed over and over again by waves, water, and weather for millions of years.

Some of the white-sand beaches of Hawaii are made from the POOP of parrotfish!

Volcanoes and shifting plates of earth (called tectonic plates) can form new islands and mountain ranges.

More people have stepped on the moon than visited the bottom of the Marianas Trench, at around 36,000 feet below the ocean's surface!

The sperm whale's rib cage and lungs deflate, allowing it to hunt for giant squid in dark depths of 7,000 or more feet.

Sunlight has a hard time traveling more than 650 feet into the ocean!

The Great Barrier Reef is so large it can be seen from space!

And just as the oceans affect
everyone everywhere, everything
we do affects the oceans.

The baths we take,
the toilets we flush,
the garbage we toss,
the balloons we let
slip from our fingers.

For a long time no one thought about how much stuff
we put in the oceans or how many fish
(and other marine life) we took out.

Sometimes it takes a while
to learn from your mistakes, right?
So now's our chance.

Because even the smallest
action can do some good.

That good deed of yours can have a great effect.
If everyone does something small to help our oceans,
those deeds will ripple outward the same way that
streams feed into creeks and brooks and rivers
and lakes, all of which eventually flow into the ocean.

This ocean of good deeds surrounds us all,
bringing everyone and everything together.

Even you,
no matter where you are.

So don't worry if you're not visiting the beach anytime soon.
The ocean's bound to visit you anyway.

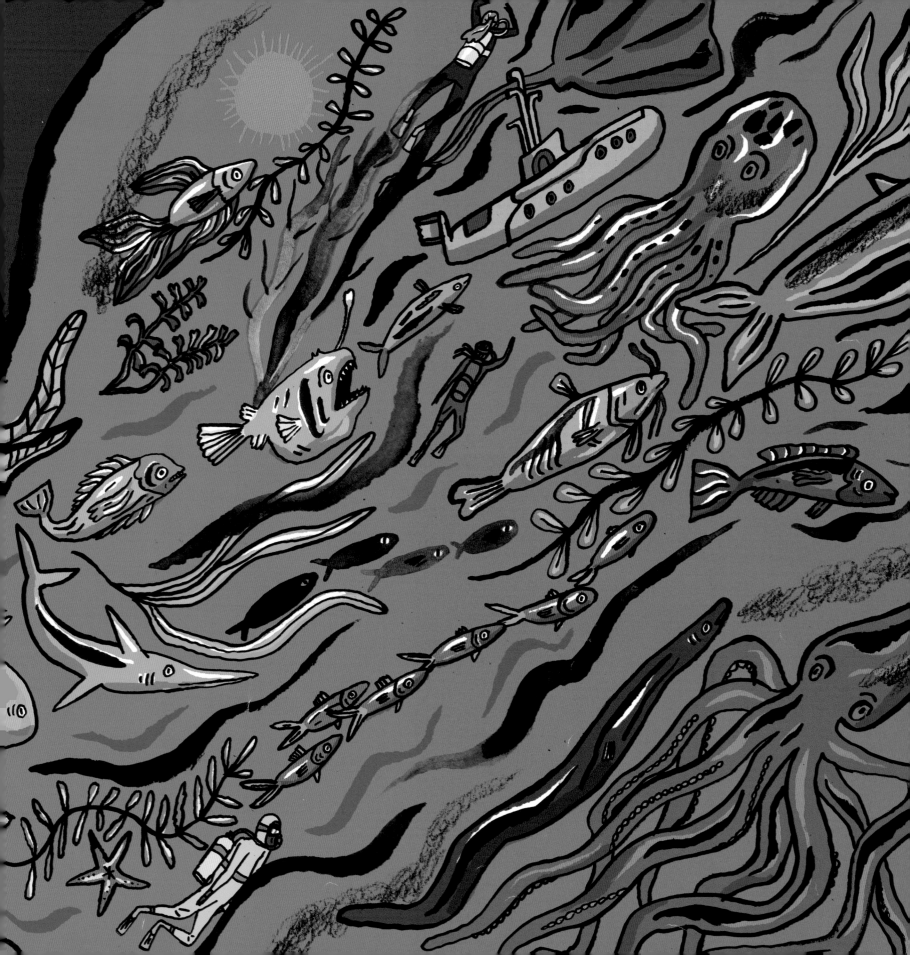

AUTHOR'S NOTE

The hardest part of writing this book was not being able to tell you *every single thing* about the ocean. The ocean is full of fascinating environmental processes, incredible geological features, and amazing creatures. But even some of what this book *did* show you deserves further explanation.

PHYTOPLANKTON

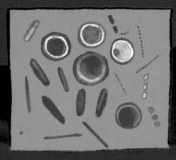

Remember that "forest" of tiny plants floating in the ocean? Those are called phytoplankton. Phytoplankton are the key to the ocean's lungs. Seaweed and other plant life help, but these microscopic plants produce most of the oxygen on Earth. And sometimes we humans affect the phytoplankton in a negative way. Farmers, to help their crops grow, often use fertilizers—such as cow poop—that contain compounds called nitrates. When fertilizers run off in rivers and spill into the ocean, those nitrates also fertilize the phytoplankton. The phytoplankton grow so fast that in some cases, their blooms of color are visible from space, and are so thick they can block the sun, which can kill all plant life beneath the surface of the water. Without plant life, the oxygen in the water depletes. Other marine life can't survive in water that doesn't have oxygen, and these areas become what are called "dead zones." One dead zone, covering almost 9,000 square miles, is in the Gulf of Mexico, where the Mississippi River meets the sea.

WATER CYCLE

The ocean provides much of our fresh water, and the water cycle is the process of filtering the salty ocean water and converting it into drinkable fresh water for our forests, animals, and for us humans. Most people think there are four steps to the water cycle, though some believe there are up to seven! To begin, salty ocean water **evaporates**, or turns from a liquid into a gas or vapor. That happens when the water near the surface gets warm enough. Then, the gas or vapor **condenses** back into a liquid in the form of a cloud. When the clouds become heavy enough, the liquid **precipitates** and falls back to earth. This is the clean rainfall we're looking for! Finally, that water becomes **runoff** and percolates, forming rivers and lakes and underground aquifers where fresh water is stored. This water evaporates again, from the ocean and the rivers and even the trees after a heavy rainfall, and the water cycle repeats.

AQUIFERS

The water from rainfall feeds plant life and goes into streams, rivers, lakes, and eventually flows back to the oceans. But it also soaks into the ground way below the roots of trees, into aquifers. Aquifers are underground layers of rock that water can pass through. This groundwater can be pulled up by wells to support crops and animals, and it is essential to the survival of humans throughout the world. Of course, the less it rains, and the more we pull from our aquifers, the emptier they become. We have to do a better job protecting our potable (that means drinkable) water.

Well

Aquifer

YOUR PART

The oceans are just begging for someone like you to learn more about them. That means playing on their shores and swimming their depths, exploring aquariums, and studying marine life. Climate change is affecting and will continue to affect the oceans as we know them. Temperatures are warming, waters are rising, and sea life is shifting. We need people like YOU to learn and understand and change with it. Right now, the oceans are protecting you, no matter where you are. Let's return the favor.